IN WEST KERRY

In West Kerry

JOHN M. SYNGE

THE MERCIER PRESS

DUBLIN and CORK

The Mercier Press Ltd
4 Bridge Street, Cork
25 Lower Abbey Street, Dublin 1

This edition © The Mercier Press, 1979

ISBN 0 85342 582 5

Printed by Litho Press Co., Midleton, Co. Cork.

PUBLISHERS NOTE

In West Kerry was partly re-written from articles which appeared in the *Shanachie* and was printed in book form under the title *In Wicklow, West Kerry and Connemara. In Connemara* is also available in a Mercier paperback.

At Tralee station—I was on my way to a village many miles beyond Dingle—I found a boy who carried my bag some way along the road to an open yard where the light railway starts for the west. There was a confused mass of peasants struggling on the platform, with all sort of baggage, which the people lifted into the train for themselves as well as they were able. The seats ran up either side of the cars, and the space between them was soon filled with sacks of flour, cases of porter, chairs rolled in straw, and other household goods. A drunken young man got in just before we started, and sang songs for a few coppers, telling us that he had spent all his money, and had nothing left to pay for his ticket. Then, when the carriage was closely packed, we moved slowly out of the station. At my side there was an old man who explained the Irish names of the places that we came to, and pointed out the Seven Pigs, a group of islands in the bay; Kerry Head, further off; and many distant mountains. Beyond him a dozen big women in shawls were crowded together; and just opposite me there was a young woman

wearing a wedding ring, who was one of the
peculiarly refined women of Kerry, with supreme
charm in every movement and expression. The
big woman talked to her about some elderly
man who had been sick—her husband, it was
likely—and some young man who had gone away
to England, and was breaking his heart with
loneliness.

'Ah, poor fellow!' she said; 'I suppose he will
get used to it like another; and wouldn't he be
worse off if he was beyond the seas in Saint
Louis, or the towns of America?'

This woman seemed to unite the healthiness
of the country people with the greatest sensitive-
ness, and whenever there was any little stir or
joke in the carriage, her face and neck flushed
with pleasure and amusement. As we went on
there were superb sights—first on the north,
towards Loop Head, and then when we reached
the top of the ridge, to the south also, to Drung
Hill, Macgillicuddy's Reeks, and other mountains of South Kerry. A little further on, nearly
all the people got out at a small station; and the
young woman I had admired gathered up most
of the household goods and got down also, lift-
ing heavy boxes with the power of a man. Then
two returned American girls got in, fine, stout-

looking women, with distress in their expression, and we started again. Dingle Bay could now be seen through narrow valleys on our left, and had extraordinary beauty in the evening light. In the carriage next to ours a number of herds and jobbers were travelling, and for the last hour they kept up a furious altercation that seemed always on the verge of breaking out into a dangerous quarrel, but no blows were given.

At the end of the line an old blue side-car was waiting to take me to the village where I was going. I was some time fastening on my goods, with the raggedy boy who was to drive me; and then we set off, passing through the usual streets of a Kerry town, with public-houses at the corners, till we left the town by a narrow quay with a few sailing boats and a small steamer with coal. Then we went over a bridge near a large water-mill, where a number of girls were standing about, with black shawls over their heads, and turned sharp to the right, against the face of the mountains. At first we went up hill for several miles, and got on slowly, though the boy jumped down once or twice and gathered a handful of switches to beat the tall mare he was driving. Just as the twilight was beginning to deepen we reached the top of the ridge and

came out through a gap into sight of Smerwick
Harbour, a wild bay with magnificent headlands
beyond it, and a long stretch of the Atlantic. We
drove on towards the west, sometimes very
quickly, where the slope was gradual, and then
slowly again when the road seemed to fall away
under us, like the wall of a house. As the night fell
the sea became like a piece of white silver on our
right; and the mountains got black on our left,
and heavy night smells began to come up out of
the bogs. Once or twice I noticed a blue cloud
over the edge of the road, and then I saw that
we were nearly against the gables of a little
village, where the houses were so closely packed
together there was no light from any of them. It
was now quite dark, and the boy got cautious in
his driving, pulling the car almost into the ditch
once or twice to avoid an enormous cavity
where the middle of the road had settled down
into the bogs. At last we came to another river
and a public-house, and went up a hill, from
which we could see the outline of a chapel; then
the boy turned to me: 'Is it ten o'clock yet?' he
said; 'for we're mostly now in the village.'

This morning, a Sunday, rain was threatening;
but I went out west after my breakfast under
Croagh Martin, in the direction of the Atlantic.

At one of the first villages I came to I had a long talk with a man who was sitting on the ditch waiting till it was time for Mass. Before long we began talking about the Irish language.

'A few years ago,' he said, 'they were all for stopping it off; and when I was a boy they tied a gobban into my mouth for the whole afternoon because I was heard speaking Irish. Wasn't that great cruelty? And now when I hear the same busybodies coming around and telling us for the love of God to speak nothing but Irish, I've a good mind to tell them to go to hell. There was a priest out here a while since who was telling us to stay always where we are, and to speak nothing but Irish; but, I suppose, although the priests are learned men, and great scholars, they don't understand the life of the people the same as another man would. In this place the land is poor—you can see that for yourself—and the people have little else to live on; so that when there is a long family, one son will stay at home and keep on the farm, and the others will go away because they must go. Then when they once pass out of the Dingle station in Tralee they won't hear a word of Irish, or meet anyone who'd understand it; so what good, I ask you, is a man who hasn't got the English, and plenty of it?'

After I left him I went on towards Dunquin,
and lay for a long time on the side of a magnificently wild road under Croagh Martin, where I
could see the Blasket Islands and the end of
Dunmore Head, the most westerly point of
Europe. It was a grey day with a curious silence
on the sea and sky and no sign of life anywhere,
except the sail of one curagh—or niavogue, as
they are called here—that was sailing in from the
islands. Now and then a cart passed me filled
with old people and children, who saluted me in
Irish; then I turned back myself. I got on a long
road running through a bog, with a smooth
mountain on one side and the sea on the other,
and Brandon in front of me, partly covered with
clouds. As far as I could see there were little
groups of people on their way to the chapel in
Ballyferriter, the men in homespun and the
women wearing blue cloaks, or, more often,
black shawls twisted over their heads. This pro-
cession along the olive bogs, between the mountains and the sea, on this grey day of autumn,
seemed to wring me with the pang of emotion
one meets everywhere in Ireland—an emotion
that is partly local and patriotic, and partly a
share of the desolation that is mixed everywhere

with the supreme beauty of the world.

In the evening, when I was walking about the village, I fell in with a man who could read Gaelic, and was full of enthusiasm for the old language and of contempt for English.

'I can tell you,' he said, 'that the English I have is no more good to me than the cover of that pipe. Buyers come here from Dingle and Cork and Clare, and they have good Irish, and so has everyone we meet with, for there is no one can do business in this place who hasn't the language on his tongue.'

Then I asked him about the young men who go away to America.

'Many go away,' he said, 'who could stay if they wished to, for it is a fine place for fishing, and a man will get more money and better health for himself, and rear a better family, in this place than in many another. It's a good place to be in, and now, with the help of God, the little children will all learn to read and write in Irish, and that is a great thing, for how can people do any good, or make a song even, if they cannot write? You will be often three weeks making a song, and there will be times when you will think of good things to put into it

that could never be beaten in the whole world;
but if you cannot write them down you will
forget them, maybe, by the next day, and then
what good will be your song?'

After a while we went upstairs to a large room
in the inn, where a number of young men and
girls were dancing jigs and reels. These young
people, although they are as Irish-speaking as the
people of Connemara, are pushing forward in
their ways of living and dress; so that this group
of dancers could hardly have been known, by
their appearance, from any Sunday party in
Limerick or Cork. After a long four-hand reel,
my friend, who was dressed in homespun,
danced a jig to the whistling of a young man
with great energy and spirit. Then he sat down
beside me in the corner, and we talked about
spring trawling and the price of nets. I told him
about the ways of Aran and Connemara; and
then he told me about the French trawlers who
come to this neighbourhood in April and May.

'The Frenchmen from Fécamp,' he said, 'are
Catholics and decent people; but those who
come from Boulogne have no religion, and are
little better than a wild beast would lep on you
out of a wood. One night there was a drift of
them below in the public-house, where there is a

counter, as you've maybe seen, with a tin top on
it. Well, they were talking together, and they
had some little difference among themselves,
and from that they went on raising their voices,
till one of them out with his knife and drove it
down through the tin into the wood! Wasn't
that a dangerous fellow?'

Then he told me about their tobacco.

'The French do have two kinds of tobacco;
one of them is called hay-tobacco, and if you
give them a few eggs, or maybe nine little
cabbage plants, they'll give you as much of it as
would fill your hat. Then we get a pound of our
own tobacco and mix the two of them together,
and put them away in a pig's bladder—it's that
way we keep our tobacco—and we have enough
with that lot for the whole winter.'

This evening a circus was advertised in Dingle,
for one night only; so I made my way there
towards the end of the afternoon, although the
weather was windy and threatening. I reached
the town an hour too soon, so I spent some time
watching the wild-looking fishermen and fishwomen who stand about the quays. Then I
wandered up and saw the evening train coming
in with the usual number of gaily-dressed young

women and half-drunken jobbers and merchants;
and at last, about eight o'clock, I went to the
circus field, just above the town, in a heavy
splash of rain. The tent was set up in the middle
of the field, and a little to the side of it a large
crowd was struggling for tickets at one of the
wheeled houses in which the acrobats live. I
went round the tent in the hope of getting in by
some easier means, and found a door in the
canvas, where a man was calling out: 'Tickets,
or money, this way,' and I passed in through a
long winding passage. It was some time after the
hour named for the show, but although the tent
was almost filled there was no sign of the performers; so I stood back in a corner and watched
the crowd coming in wet and dripping from the
rain, which had turned to a downpour. The tent
was lighted by a few flaring gas-jets round the
central pole, with an opening above them,
through which the rain shot down in straight
whistling lines. The top of the tent was dripping
and saturated, and the gas, shining sideways
across, made it glitter in many places with the
brilliancy of golden silk. When a sudden squall
came with a rush from the narrow valleys
behind the town, the whole structure billowed,
and flapped and strained, till one waited every

moment to see the canvas fall upon our heads.
The people, who looked strangely black and
swarthy in the uncertain light, were seated all
round on three or four rows of raised wooden
seats, and many who were late were still crush-
ing forward, and standing in dense masses
wherever there was room. At the entrance a
rather riotous crowd began to surge in so quickly that there was some danger of the place being
rushed. Word was sent across the ring, and in a
moment three or four of the women performers,
with long streaming ulsters buttoned over their
tights, ran out from behind the scenes and threw
themselves into the crowd, forcing back the wild
hillside people, fishwomen and drunken sailors,
in an extraordinary tumult of swearing, wrestling
and laughter. These women seemed to enjoy this
part of their work, and shrieked with amusement when two or three of them fell on some
enormous farmer or publican and nearly dragged
him to the ground. Here and there among the
people I could see a little party of squireens and
their daughters, in the fashions of five years ago,
trying, not always successfully, to reach the
shilling seats. The crowd was now so thick I
could see little more than the heads of the
performers, who had at last come into the ring,

and many of the shorter women who were near
me must have seen nothing the whole evening,
yet they showed no sign of impatience. The
performance was begun by the usual dirty white
horse, that was brought out and set to gallop
round, with a gaudy horse-woman on his back
who jumped through a hoop and did the
ordinary feats, the horse's hoofs splashing and
possing all the time in the green slush of the ring.
An old door-mat was laid down near the entrance
for the performers, and as they came out in turn
they wiped the mud from their feet before they
got up on their horses. A little later the clown came
out, to the great delight of the people. He was
followed by some gymnasts, and then the horse-
people came out again in different dress and
make-up, and went through their old turns once
more. After that there was prolonged fooling
between the clown and the chief horseman, who
made many medieval jokes, that reminded me of
little circuses on the outer Boulevards of Paris,
and at last the horseman sang a song which won
great applause:—

> Here's to the man who kisses his wife,
> And kisses his wife alone;
> For there's many a man kissed another
> > man's wife

When he thought he kissed his own.

Here's to the man who rocks his child,
And rocks his child alone;
For there's many a man rocked another
                        man's child
When he thought he rocked his own.

About ten o'clock there seemed to be a lull in the storm, so I went out into the open air with two young men who were going the road I had to travel. The rain had stopped for a moment, but a high wind was blowing as we made our way to a public-house to get a few biscuits and a glass of beer before we started. A sleepy barmaid, who was lolling behind the counter with a novel pricked up her ears when she heard us talking of our journey.

'Surely you are not going to Ballydavid,' she said, 'at such an hour of a night like this.'

We told her we were going to a place which was further away.

'Well,' she said, 'I wouldn't go to that place tonight if you had a coach-and-four to drive me in, and gave me twenty pounds into the bargain! How at all will you get on in the darkness when the roads will be running with water, and you'll be likely to slip down every place into some drain or ditch?'

When we went out, and began to make our
way down the steep hill through the town, the
night seemed darker than ever after the glare of
the bar. Before we had gone many yards a
woman's voice called out sharply from under the
wall: 'Mind the horse.' I looked up and saw the
black outline of a horse's head standing right
above me. It was not plain in such darkness how
we should get to the end of our ten-mile journey;
but one of the young men borrowed a lantern
from a chandler in the bottom of the town, and
we made our way over the bridge and up the
hill, going slowly and painfully with just light
enough, when we kept close together, to avoid
the sloughs of water and piles of stones on the
roadway. By the time we reached the top of the
ridge and began to work down carefully towards
Smerwick, the rain stopped, and we reached the
village without any mishap.

I go out often in the mornings to the site of
Sybil Ferriter's Castle, on a little headland
reached by a narrow strip of rocks. As I lie there
I can watch whole flights of cormorants and
choughs and seagulls that fly about under the
cliffs, and beyond them a number of niavogues
that are nearly always fishing in Ferriter's Cove.

Further on there are Sybil Head and three rocky points, the Three Sisters; then Smerwick Harbour and Brandon far away, usually covered with white airy clouds. Between these headlands and the village there is a strip of sandhill grown over with sea-holly, and a low beach where scores of red bullocks lie close to the sea, or wade in above their knees. Further on one passes peculiar horseshoe coves, with contorted lines of sandstone on one side and slaty blue rocks on the other, and necks of transparent sea of wonderful blueness between them.

I walked up this morning along the slope from the east to the top of Sybil Head, where one comes out suddenly on the brow of a cliff with a straight fall of many hundred feet into the sea. It is a place of indescribable grandeur, where one can see Carrantuohill and the Skelligs and Loop Head and the full sweep of the Atlantic, and, over all, the wonderfully tender and searching light that is seen only in Kerry. Looking down the drop of five or six hundred feet, the height is so great that the gannets flying close over the sea look like white butterflies, and the choughs like flies fluttering behind them. One wonders in these places why anyone is left in Dublin, or London, or Paris, when it would be better, one

would think, to live in a tent or hut with this
magnificent sea and sky, and to breathe this
wonderful air, which is like wine in one's teeth.

Here and there on this headland there are
little villages of ten or twenty houses, closely
packed together without any order or roadway.
Usually there are one or two curious beehive-
like structures in these villages, used here, it is
said, as pig-styes or storehouses. On my way
down from Sybil Head I was joined by a tall
young man, who told me he had been in the
navy, but had bought himself out before his
time was over.

'Twelve of us joined from this place,' he said,
'and I was the last of them that stayed in it, for
it is a life that no one could put up with. It's not
the work that would trouble you, but it's that
they can't leave you alone, and that you must
be ever and always fooling over something.'

He had been in South Africa during the war,
and in Japan, and all over the world; but he was
now dressed in homespuns, and had settled
down here, he told me, for the rest of his life.
Before we reached the village we met Maurice,
the fisherman I have spoken of, and we sat down
under a hedge to shelter from a shower. We
began to talk of fevers and sicknesses and

doctors — these little villages are often infested with typhus — and Maurice spoke about the traditional cures.

'There is a plant,' he said, 'which is the richest that is growing out of the ground, and in the old times the women used to be giving it to their children till they'd be growing up seven feet maybe in height. Then the priests and doctors began taking everything to themselves and destroyed the old knowledge, and that is a poor thing; for you know well it was the Holy Mother of God who cured her own Son with plants the like of that, and said after that no mother should be without a plant for ever to cure her child. Then she threw out the seeds of it over the whole world, so that it's growing every place from that day to this.'

I came out today, a holiday, to the great Blasket Island with a schoolmaster and two young men from the village, who were coming for the afternoon only. The day was admirably clear, with a blue sea and sky, and the voyage in the long canoe — I had not been in one for two or three years — gave me indescribable enjoyment. We passed Dunmore Head, and then stood out nearly due west towards the Great Blasket itself, the height of the mountains round the bay and the sharpness of the rocks making the place singularly different from the sounds about Aran, where I had last travelled in a curagh. As usual, three men were rowing — the man I have come to stay with, his son, and a tall neighbour, all dressed in blue jerseys, homespun trousers and shirts, and talking in Irish only, though my host could speak good English when he chose to. As we came nearer the island, which seemed to rise like a mountain straight out of the sea, we could make out a crowd of people in their holiday clothes standing or sitting along the brow of the cliff watching our approach, and just beyond them a patch of cottages with roofs of tarred felt. A little later we doubled into a cove among the rocks, where I landed at a boat slip, and then scrambled up a steep zig-zag pathway to the head of the cliff, where the people crowded round us and shook hands with the men who had come with me.

This cottage where I am to stay is one of the highest of the group, and as we passed up to it through little paths among the cottages many white, wolfish-looking dogs came out and barked furiously. My host had gone on in front with my bag, and when I reached his threshold

he came forward and shook hands with me
again, with a finished speech of welcome. His
eldest daughter, a young married woman of
about twenty, who manages the house, shook
hands with me also, and then, without asking if
we were hungry, began making us tea in a metal
teapot and frying rashers of bacon. She is a
small, beautifully-formed woman, with brown
hair and eyes - instead of the black hair and
blue eyes that are usually found with this type
in Ireland - and delicate feet and ankles that are
not common in these parts, where the woman's
work is so hard. Her sister, who lives in the
house also, is a bonny girl of about eighteen, full
of humour and spirits.

The schoolmaster made many jokes in English
and Irish while the little hostess served our tea;
and then the kitchen filled up with young men
and women — the men dressed like ordinary
fishermen, the women wearing print bodices and
coloured skirts, that had none of the distinction
of the dress of Aran — and a polka was danced,
with curious solemnity, in a whirl of dust. When
it was over it was time for my companions to go
back to the mainland. As soon as we came out
and began to go down to the sea, a large crowd,
made up of nearly all the men and women and

children of the island, came down also, closely
packed round us. At the edge of the cliff the
young men and the schoolmaster bade me good-
bye and went down the zig-zag path, leaving me
alone with the islanders on the ledge of rock,
where I had seen the people as we came in. I sat
for a long time watching the sail of the canoe
moving away to Dunquin, and talking to a
young man who had spent some years in Ballyferriter, and had good English. The evening was
peculiarly fine, and after a while, when the
crowd had scattered, I passed up through the
cottages, and walked through a boreen towards
the north-west, between a few plots of potatoes
and little fields of weeds that seemed to have
gone out of cultivation not long ago. Beyond
these I turned up a sharp, green hill, and came
out suddenly on the broken edge of a cliff. The
effect was wonderful. The Atlantic was right
underneath; then I could see the sharp rocks of
several uninhabited islands, a mile or two off,
the Tearaught further away, and, on my left, the
whole northern edge of this island curving round
towards the west, with a steep heathery face, a
thousand feet high. The whole sight of wild
islands and sea was as clear and cold and brilliant
as what one sees in a dream, and alive with the

singularly severe glory that is in the character of
this place.

As I was wandering about I saw many of the
younger islanders, not far off, jumping and putting
the weight — a heavy stone — or running races
on the grass. Then four girls, walking arm-in-arm,
came up and talked to me in Irish. Before long
they began to laugh loudly at some signs I made
to eke out my meaning, and by degrees the men
wandered up also, till there was a crowd round
us. The cold of the night was growing stronger,
however, and we soon turned back to the village,
and sat round the fire in the kitchen the rest of
the evening.

At eleven o'clock the people got up as one
man and went away, leaving me with the little
hostess — the man of the house had gone to the
mainland with the young men — her husband
and sister. I told them I was sleepy, and ready to
go to bed; so the little hostess lighted a candle,
carried it into the room beyond the kitchen,
and stuck it up on the end of the bed-post of
one of the beds with a few drops of grease. Then
she took off her apron, and fastened it up in the
window as a blind, laid another apron on the
wet earthen floor for me to stand on, and left
me to myself. The room had two beds, running

from wall to wall with a small space between them, a chair that the little hostess had brought in, an old hair-brush that was propping the window open, and no other article. When I had been in bed for some time, I heard the host's voice in the kitchen, and a moment or two later he came in with a candle in his hand, and made a long apology for having been away the whole of my first evening on the island, holding the candle while he talked very close to my face. I told him I had been well entertained by his family and neighbours, and had hardly missed him. He went away, and half an hour later opened the door again with the iron spoon which serves to lift the latch, and came in, in a suit of white homespuns, and said he must ask me to let him stretch out in the other bed, as there was no place else for him to lie. I told him that he was welcome, and he got into the other bed and lit his pipe. Then we had a long talk about this place and America and the younger generations.

'There has been no one drowned on this island,' he said, 'for forty years, and that is a great wonder, for it is a dangerous life. There was a man — the brother of the man you were talking to when the girls were dancing — was

married to a widow had a public-house away to
the west of Bally'david, and he was out fishing
for mackerel, and he got a great haul of them;
then he filled his canoe too full, so that she was
down to the edge in the water, and a wave broke
into her when they were near the shore, and she
went down under them. Two men got ashore,
but the man from this island was drowned, for
his oilskins went down about his feet, and he
sank where he was.'

Then we talked about the chances of the
mackerel season. 'If the season is good,' he said,
'we get on well; but it is not certain at all. We do
pay £4 for a net, and sometimes the dogfish will
get into it the first day and tear it into pieces as
if you'd cut it with a knife. Sometimes the
mackerel will die in the net, and then ten men
would he hard set to pull them up into the
canoe, so that if the wind rises on us we must
cut loose, and let down the net to the bottom of
the sea. When we get fish here in the night we go
to Dunquin and sell them to buyers in the morning; and, believe me, it is a dangerous thing to
cross that sound when you have too great a load
taken into your canoe. When it is too bad to
cross over we do salt the fish ourselves — we
must salt them cleanly and put them in clean

barrels — and then the first day it is calm buyers
will be out after them from the town of Dingle.

Afterwards he spoke of the people who go
away to America, and the younger generations
that are growing up now in Ireland.

'The young people is no use,' he said. 'I am
not as good a man as my father was, and my son
is growing up worse than I am.' Then he put up
his pipe on the end of the bed-post. 'You'll be
tired now,' he went on, 'so it's time we were
sleeping; and, I humbly beg your pardon, might
I ask your name?' I told him.

'Well, good night so,' he said, 'and may you
have a good sleep your first night in this island.'

Then he put out the candle and we settled
to sleep. In a few minutes I could hear that he
was in his dreams, and just as my own ideas were
beginning to wander the house door opened, and
the son of the place, a young man of about
twenty, came in and walked into our room,
close to my bed, with another candle in his
hand. I lay with my eyes closed, and the young
man did not seem pleased with my presence,
though he looked at me with curiosity. When he
was satisfied he went back to the kitchen, and
took a drink of whisky and said his prayers;
then, after loitering about for some time and

playing with a little mongrel greyhound that seemed to adore him, he took off his clothes, clambered over his father, and stretched out on the inner side of the bed.

I awoke in the morning about six o'clock, and not long afterwards the host awoke also, and asked how I did. Then he wanted to know if I ever drank whisky; and when he heard that I did so, he began calling for one of his daughters at the top of his voice. In a few moments the younger girl came in, her eyes closing with sleep, and, at the host's bidding, got the whisky bottle, some water, and a green wine-glass out of the kitchen. She came first to my bedside and gave me a dram, then she did the same for her father and brother, handed us our pipes and tobacco, and went back to the kitchen.

There were to be sports at noon in Ballyferriter, and when we had talked for a while I asked the host if he would think well of my going over to see them. 'I would not,' he said; 'you'd do better to stay quiet in this place where you are; the men will be all drunk coming back, fighting and kicking in the canoes, and a man the like of you, who aren't used to us, would be frightened. Then, if you went, the people would be taking you into one public-house, and then into another, till you'd maybe get drunk yourself, and that wouldn't be a nice thing for a gentleman. Stay where you are in this island and you'll be safest so.'

When the son got up later and began going in and out of the kitchen, some of the neighbours, who had already come in, stared at me with curiosity as I lay in my bed; then I got up myself and went into the kitchen. The little hostess set about getting my breakfast, but before it was ready she partly rinsed the dough out of a pan where she had been kneading bread, poured some water into it, and put it on a chair near the door. Then she hunted about the edges of the rafters till she found a piece of soap, which she put on the back of a chair with the towel, and told me I might wash my face. I did so as well as I was able, in the middle of the people, and dried myself with the towel, which was the one used by the whole family.

The morning looked as if it would turn to rain and wind, so I took the advice I had been given and let the canoes go off without me to the sports. After a turn on the cliffs I came back to the house to write letters. The little hostess was washing up the breakfast things when I arrived

with my papers and pens, but she made room
for me at the table, and spread out an old news-
paper for me to write on. A little later, when she
had finished her washing, she came over to her
usual place in the chimney corner, not far from
where I was sitting, sat down on the floor, and
took out her hairpins and began combing her
hair. As I finished each letter I had to say who it
was to, and where the people lived; and then I
had to tell her if they were married or single,
how many children they had, and make a guess
at how many pounds they spent in the year, and
at the number of their servants. Just before I
finished, the younger girl came back with three
or four other young women, who were followed
in a little while by a party of men.

I showed them some photographs of the Aran
Islands and Wicklow, which they looked at with
eagerness. The little hostess was especially taken
with two or three that had babies or children
in their foreground; and as she put her hands on
my shoulders, and leaned over to look at them,
with the confidence that is so usual in these
places, I could see that she had her full share of
the passion for children which is powerful in all
women who are permanently and profoundly
attractive. While I was telling her what I could

about the children, I saw one of the men looking
with peculiar amazement at an old photograph
of myself that had been taken many years ago in
an alley of the Luxembourg Gardens, where
there were many statues in the background.
'Look at that,' he whispered in Irish to one of
the girls, pointing to the statues; 'in those
countries they do have naked people standing
about in their skins.'

I explained that the figures were of marble
only, and then the little hostess and all the girls
examined them also. 'Oh! dear me,' said the
little hostess, 'Is deas an rud do bheith ag siubhal
ins an domhain mor' ('It's a fine thing to be
travelling in the big world').

In the afternoon I went up and walked along
the narrow central ridge of the island, till I came
to the highest point, which is nearly three miles
west of the village. The weather was gloomy and
wild, and there was something nearly appalling
in the loneliness of the place. I could look down
on either side into a foggy edge of grey moving
sea, and then further off I could see many
distant mountains, or look out across the
shadowy outline of Inishtooskert to the Tearaught rock. While I was sitting on the little
mound which marks the summit of the island —

a mound stripped and riddled by rabbits — a
heavy bank of fog began to work up from the
south, behind Valentia, on the other jaw of
Dingle Bay. As soon as I saw it I hurried down
from the pinnacle where I was, so that I might
get away from the more dangerous locality
before the cloud overtook me. In spite of my
haste I had not gone half a mile when an edge of
fog whisked and circled round me, and in a
moment I could see nothing but a grey shroud
of mist and a few yards of steep, slippery grass.
Everything was distorted and magnified to an
extraordinary degree; but I could hear the moan
of the sea under me, and I knew my direction,
so I worked along towards the village without
trouble. In some places the island, on this southern side, is bitten into by sharp, narrow coves,
and when the fog opened a little I could see
across them, where gulls and choughs were
picking about on the grass, looking as big as
Kerry cattle or black mountain sheep. Before
I reached the house the cloud had turned to a
sharp shower of rain, and as I went in the water
was dripping from my hat. 'Oh! dear me,' said
the little hostess, when she saw me, 'Ta tu an-
rhluc anois' ('You are very wet now'). She was
alone in the house, breathing audibly, with a

sort of simple self-importance, as she washed her
jugs and teacups. While I was drinking my tea, a
little later, some women came in with three or
four little girls — the most beautiful children I
have ever seen — who live in one of the nearest
cottages. They tried to get the little girls to
dance a reel together, but the smallest of them
went and hid her head in the skirts of the little
hostess. In the end two of the little girls danced
with two of those who were grown up, to the
lilting of one of them. The little hostess sat at
the fire while they danced, plucking and drawing
a cormorant for the men's dinner, and calling
out to the girls when they lost the step of the
dance.

In the evenings of Sundays and holidays the
young men and girls go out to a rocky headland
on the north-west, where there is a long, grassy
slope, to dance and amuse themselves; and this
evening I wandered out there with two men,
telling them ghost stories in Irish as we went.
When we turned over the edge of the hill we
came on a number of young men lying on the
short grass playing cards. We sat down near
them, and before long a party of girls and young
women came up also and sat down, twenty

paces off, on the brink of the cliff, some of them wearing the fawn-coloured shawls that are so attractive and so much thought of in the south. It was just after sunset, and Inishtooskert was standing out with a smoky blue outline against the redness of the sky. At the foot of the cliff a wonderful silvery light was shining on the sea, which already, before the beginning of autumn, was eager and wintry and cold. The little group of blue-coated men lying on the grass, and the group of girls further off, had a singular effect in this solitude of rocks and sea; and in spite of their high spirits it gave me a sort of grief to feel the utter loneliness and desolation of the place that has given these people their finest qualities.

One of the young men had been thrown from a car a few days before on his way home from Dingle, and his face was still raw and bleeding and horrible to look at; but the young girls seemed to find romance in his condition, and several of them went over and sat in a group round him, stroking his arms and face. When the card-playing was over I showed the young men a few tricks and feats, which they worked at themselves, to the great amusement of of the girls, till they had accomplished them all.

On our way back to the village the young girls
ran wild in the twilight, flying and shrieking over
the grass, or rushing up behind the young men
and throwing them over, if they were able, by a
sudden jerk or trip. The men in return caught
them by one hand, and spun them round and
round four or five times, and then let them go,
when they whirled down the grassy slope for
many yards, spinning like peg-tops, and only
keeping their feet by the greatest efforts or
good-luck.

When we got to the village the people scattered for supper, and in our cottage the little
hostess swept the floor and sprinkled it with
some sand she had brought home in her apron.
Then she filled a crock with drinking water, lit
the lamp and sat down by the fire to comb her
hair. Some time afterwards, when a number of
young men had come in, as was usual, to spend
the evening, some one said a niavogue was on its
way home from the sports. We went out to the
door, but it was too dark to see anything except
the lights of a little steamer that was passing up
the sound, almost beneath us, on its way to
Limerick or Tralee. When it had gone by we
could hear a furious drunken uproar coming up
from a canoe that was somewhere out in the

bay. It sounded as if the men were strangling or murdering each other, and it seemed almost miraculous that they should be able to manage their canoe. The people seemed to think they were in no special danger, and we went in again to the fire and talked about porter and whisky (I have never heard the men here talk for half an hour of anything without some allusion to drink), discussing how much a man could drink with comfort in a day, whether it is better to drink when a man is thirsty or at ordinary times, and what food gives the best liking for porter. Then they asked me how much porter I could drink myself, and I told them I could drink whisky, but that I had no taste for porter, and would only take a pint or two at odd times, when I was thirsty.

'The girls are laughing to hear you say that,' said an old man; 'but whisky is a lighter drink, and I'd sooner have it myself, and any old man would say the same.' A little later some young men came in, in their Sunday clothes, and told us the news of the sports.

This morning it was raining heavily, and the host got out some nets and set to work with his son and son-in-law, mending many holes that

had been cut by dogfish, as the mackerel season
is soon to begin. While they were at work the
kitchen emptied and filled continually with
islanders passing in and out, and discussing the
weather and the season. Then they started
cutting each other's hair, the man who was being
cut sitting with an oilskin round him on a little
stool by the door, and some other men came in
to sharpen their razors on the host's razor-strop,
which seems to be the only one on the island. I
had not shaved since I arrived, so the little
hostess asked me after a while if I would like to
shave myself before dinner. I told her I would,
so she got me some water in the potato-dish and
put it on a chair; then her sister got me a little
piece of broken looking-glass and put it on a nail
near the door, where there was some light. I set
to work, and as I stood with my back to the
people I could catch a score of eyes in the glass,
watching me intently. 'That is a great improve-
ment to you now,' said the host, when I had
done; 'and whenever you want a beard, God
bless you, you'll have a thick one surely.'

When I was coming down in the evening from
the ridge of the island where I spent much of my
time looking at the richness of the Atlantic on
one side and the sad or shining greys of Dingle

Bay on the other, I was joined by two young
women and we walked back together. Just outside the village we met an old woman who
stopped and laughed at us. 'Well, aren't you in
good fortune this night, stranger,' she said, 'to
be walking up and down in the company of
women?'

'I am surely,' I answered; 'isn't that the best
thing to be doing in the whole world?'

At our own door I saw the little hostess
sweeping the floor, so I went down for a
moment to the gable of the cottage, and looked
out over the roofs of the little village to the
sound, where the tide was running with extraordinary force. In a few minutes the little hostess
came down and stood beside me — she thought I
should not be left by myself when I had been
driven away by the dust — and I asked her many
questions about the names and relationships of
the people that I am beginning to know.

Afterwards, when many of the people had
come together in the kitchen, the men told me
about their lobster-pots that are brought from
Southampton, and cost half-a-crown each. 'In
good weather,' said the man who was talking to
me, 'they will often last for a quarter; but if
storms come up on them they will sometimes

break up in a week or two. Still and all, it is a
good trade; and we do sell lobsters and crayfish
every week in the season to a boat from England
or a boat from France that does come in here, as
you'll maybe see before you go.'

I told them that I had often been in France,
and one of the boys began counting up the
numerals in French to show what he had learnt
from their buyers. A little later, when the talk
was beginning to flag, I turned to a young man
near me — the best fiddler, I was told, on the
island — and asked him to play us a dance. He
made excuses, and would not get his fiddle; but
two of the girls slipped off and brought it. The
young man tuned it and offered it to me, but I
insisted that he should take it first. Then he
played one or two tunes, without tone, but with
good intonation and rhythm. When it was my
turn I played a few tunes also; but the pitch was
so low I could not do what I wanted, and I had
not much success with the people, though the
fiddler himself watched me with interest. 'That
is great playing,' he said, when I had finished;
'and I never seen anyone the like of you for
moving your hand and getting the sound out of
it with the full drag of the bow.' Then he played
a polka and four couples danced. The women, as

usual, were in their naked feet, and whenever there was a figure for women only there was a curious hush and patter of bare feet, till the heavy pounding and shuffling of the men's boots broke in again. The whirl of music and dancing in this little kitchen stirred me with an extraordinary effect. The kindliness and merry-making of these islanders, who, one knows, are full of riot and severity and daring, has a quality and attractiveness that is absent altogether from the life of towns, and makes one think of the life that is shown in the ballads of Scotland.

After the dance the host, who had come in, sang a long English doggerel about a poor scholar who went to Maynooth and had great success in his studies, so that he was praised by the bishop. Then he went home for his holiday, and a young woman who had great riches asked him into her parlour and told him it was no fit life for a fine young man to be a priest, always saying Mass for poor people, and that he would have a right to give up his Latin and get married to herself. He refused her offers and went back to his college. When he was gone she went to the justice in great anger, and swore an oath against him that he had seduced her and left her with child. He was brought back for his trial, and he was in risk to be degraded and hanged, when a man rode up on a horse and said it was himself was the lover of the lady, and the father of her child.

Then they told me about an old man of eighty years, who is going to spend the winter alone on Inishvickillaun, an island six miles from this village. His son is making canoes and doing other carpenter's jobs on this island, and the other children have scattered also; but the old man refuses to leave the island he has spent his life on, so they have left him with a goat, and a bag of flour and stack of turf.

I have just been to the weaver's, looking at his loom and appliances. The host took me down to his cottage over the brow of the village, where some young men were finishing the skeleton of a canoe; and we found his family crowded round a low table on green stools with rope seats, finishing their dinner of potatoes. A little later the old weaver, who looks pale and sickly compared with the other islanders, took me into a sort of outhouse with a damp feeling in the air, where his loom was set up. He showed me how it was worked, and then brought out some pieces of stuff that he had woven. At first I was puzzled by the fine brown colour of some of the material; but they explained it was from selected wools of the black or mottled sheep that are common here, and are so variegated that many tints of grey or brown can be had from their fleeces. The wool for the flannel is sometimes spun on this island; sometimes it is given to women in Dunquin, who spin it cheaply for so much a pound. Then it is woven, and finally the stuff is sent to a mill in Dingle to be cleaned and dressed before it is given to a tailor in Dingle to be made up for their own use. Such cloth is not cheap, but is of wonderful quality and strength. When I came out of the weaver's, a little sailing smack was anchored in the sound, and someone on board her was blowing a horn. They told me she was the French boat, and as I went back to my cottage I could see many canoes hurrying out to her with their cargoes of lobsters and crabs.

I have left the island again. I walked round the cliffs in the morning, and then packed my bag in my room, several girls putting their heads into the little window while I did so, to say it was a great pity I was not staying on for another week or a fortnight. Then the men went off with my bag in a heavy shower, and I waited a minute

or two while the little hostess buttered some
bread for my lunch, and tied it up in a clean
handkerchief of her own. Then I bid them good-
bye, and set off down to the slip with three
girls, who came with me to see that I did not go
astray among the innumerable paths. It was still
raining heavily, so I told them to put my cape,
which they were carrying, over their heads. They
did so with delight, and ran down the path
before me, to the great amusement of the islanders. At the head of the cliff many people were
standing about to bid me good-bye and wish me
a good voyage.

The wind was in our favour, so the men took
in their oars after rowing for about a quarter of
a mile and lay down in the bottom of the canoe,
while one man ran up the sail, and the host
steered with an oar. At Dunquin the host hired
me a dray, without springs, kissed my hand in
farewell, and I was driven away.

I have made my way round the foot of Dingle
Bay and up the south coast to a cottage where I
often lodge. As I was resting in a ditch sometime
in the afternoon, on a lonely mountain road, a
little girl came along with a shawl over her head.
She stopped in front of me and asked me where

I was going, and then after a little talk: 'Well, man, let you come,' she said; 'I'm going your road as well as you.' I got up and we started. When I got tired of the hill I mounted, and she ran along beside me for several miles, till we fell in with some people cutting turf, and she stopped to talk to them.

Then for a while my road ran round an immense valley of magnificent rich turf bog, with mountains all round, and bowls where hidden lakes were lying bitten out of the cliffs.

As I was resting again on a bridge over the Behy where Diarmuid caught salmon with Grania, a man stopped to light his pipe and talk to me. 'There are three lakes above,' he said 'Coomacarra, Coomaglaslaw and Coomasdhara; the whole of this place was in a great state in the bad times. Twenty years ago they sent down a 'mergency man to lodge above by the lake and serve processes on the people, but the people were off before him and lay abroad in the heather. Then, in the course of a piece, a night came, with great rain out of the heavens, and my man said: "I'll get them this night in their own beds, surely." Then he let call the peelers — they had peelers waiting to mind him — and down they come to the big stepping-stones they have

above ɪor crossing the first river coming out of
the lakes. My man going in front to cross over,
and the water was high up covering the stones.
Then he gave two leps or three, and the peelers
heard him give a great shriek down in the flood.
They went home after — what could they do? —
and the 'mergency man was found in the sea
stuck in a net.'

I was singularly pleased when I turned up the
boreen at last to this cottage where I lodge, and
looked down through a narrow gully to Dingle
Bay. The people bade me welcome when I came
in, the old woman kissing my hand.

There is no village near this cottage, yet many
farms are scattered on the hills near it; and as
the people are in some ways a leading family,
many men and women look in to talk or tell
stories, or to buy a few pennyworth of sugar or
starch. Although the main road passes a few
hundred yards to the west, this cottage is well
known also to the race of local tramps who
move from one family to another in some special
neighbourhood or barony. This evening, when I
came in, a little old man in a tall hat and long
brown coat was sitting up on the settle beside
the fire, and intending to spend, one could see, a
night or more in the place.

I had a great deal to tell the people at first of
my travels in different parts of the county, to
the Blasket Islands — which they can see from
here — Corkaguiney and Tralee; and they had
news to tell me also of people who have married
or died since I was here before, or gone away, or
come back from America. Then I was told that
the old man, Dermot (or Darby, as he is called
in English), was the finest story-teller in Iveragh;
and after a while he told us a long story in Irish,
but spoke so rapidly and indistinctly — he had
no teeth — that I could understand but few
passages. When he had finished I asked him
where he had heard the story.

'I heard it in the city of Portsmouth,' he said.
'I worked there for fifteen years, and four years
in Plymouth, and a long while in the hills of
Wales; twenty-five years in all I was working at
the other side; and there were many Irish in it,
who would be telling stories in the evening, the
same as we are doing here. I heard many good
stories, but what can I do with them now and I
an old lisping fellow, the way I can't give them
out like a ballad?'

When he had talked a little more about his
travels, and a bridge over the Severn, that he
thought the greatest wonder of the world, I

asked him if he remembered the Famine.

'I do,' he said. 'I was living near Kenmare, and many's the day I saw them burying the corpses in the ditch by the road. It was after that I went to England, for this country was ruined and destroyed. I heard there was work at that time in Plymouth; so I went to Dublin and took a boat that was going to England; but it was at a place called Liverpool they put me on shore, and then I had to walk to Plymouth, asking my way on the road. In that place I saw the soldiers after coming back from the Crimea, and they all broken and maimed.'

A little later, when he went out for a moment, the people told me he beats up and down between Killorglin and Ballinskelligs and the Inny river, and that he is a particular crabby kind of man, and will not take anything from the people but coppers and eggs.

'And he's a wasteful old fellow with all,' said the woman of the house, 'though he's eighty years old or beyond it, for whatever money he'll get one day selling his eggs to the coast-guards, he'll spend it the next getting a drink when he's thirsty, or keeping good boots on his feet.'

From that they began talking of misers, and

telling stories about them.

'There was an old woman,' said one of the men, 'living beyond to the east, and she was thought to have a great store of money. She had one daughter only, and in the course of a piece a young lad got married to her, thinking he'd have her fortune. The woman died after — God be merciful to her! — and left the two of them as poor as they were before. Well, one night a man that knew them was passing to the fair of Puck, and he came in and asked would they give him a lodging for that night. They gave him what they had and welcome; and after his tea, when they were sitting over the fire — the way we are this night — the man asked them how they were so poor-looking, and if the old woman had left nothing behind her.

' "Not a farthing did she leave," said the daughter.

' "And did she give no word or warning or message in her last moments?" said the man.

' "She did not," said the daughter, "except only that I shouldn't comb out the hair of her poll and she dead."

' "And you heeded her?" said the man.

' "I did, surely," said the daughter.

' "Well," said the man, "tomorrow night when

I'm gone let the two of you go down the Relic (the graveyard) and dig up her coffin and look in her hair and see what it is you'll find in it."

' "We'll do that," said the daughter, and with that they all stretched out for the night.

'The next evening they went down quietly with a shovel and they dug up the coffin, and combed through her hair, and there behind her poll they found her fortune, five hundred pounds, in good notes and gold.'

'There was an old fellow living on the little hill beyond the graveyard,' said Danny-boy, when the man had finished, 'and he had his fortune some place hid in his bed, and he was an old weak fellow, so that they were all watching him to see he wouldn't hide it away. One time there was no one in it but himself and a young girl, and the old fellow slipped out of his bed and went out of the door as far as a little bush and some stones. The young girl kept her eye on him, and she made sure he'd hidden something in the bush; so when he was back in his bed she called the people, and they all came and looked in the bushes, but not a thing could they find. The old man died after, and no one ever found his fortune to this day.'

'There were some young lads a while since,'

said the old woman, 'and they went up of a Sunday and began searching through those bushes to
see if they could find anything, but a kind of
turkey-cock came up out of the stones and
drove them away.'

'There was another old woman,' said the man
of the house, 'who tried to take down her
fortune into her stomach. She was near death,
and she was all day stretched in her bed at the
corner of the fire. One day when the girl was
tinkering about, the old woman rose up and got
ready a little skillet that was near the hob and
put something into it and put it down by the
fire, and the girl watching her all the time under
her oxter, not letting on she scen her at all.
When the old woman lay down again the girl
went over to put on more sods on the fire, and
she got a look into the skillet, and what did she
see but sixty sovereigns. She knew well what the
old woman was striving to do, so she went out
to the dairy and she got a lump of fresh butter
and put it down into the skillet, when the old
woman didn't see her do it at all. After a bit the
old woman rose up and looked into the skillet,
and when she saw the froth of the butter she
thought it was the gold that was melted. She got
back into her bed—a dark place, maybe—and she

began sipping and sipping the butter till she had
the whole of it swallowed. Then the girl made
some trick to entice the skillet away from her,
and she found the sixty sovereigns in the bottom
and she kept them for herself.'

By this time it was late, and the old woman
brought over a mug of milk and a piece of bread
to Darby at the settle, and the people gathered
at their table for their supper; so I went into the
little room at the end of the cottage where I am
given a bed.

When I came into the kitchen in the morning,
old Darby was still asleep on the settle, with his
coat and trousers over him, a red night-cap on his
head, and his half-bred terrier, Jess, chained
with a chain he carries with him to the leg of the
settle.

'That's a poor way to lie on the bare board,'
said the woman of the house, when she saw me
looking at him; 'but when I filled a sack with
straw for him last night he wouldn't have it at
all.'

While she was boiling some eggs for my breakfast, Darby roused up from his sleep, pulled on
his trousers and coat, slipped his feet into his
boots and started off, when he had eaten a few
mouthfuls for another house where he is known,

some five miles away.

Afterwards I went out on the cnuceen, a little hill between this cottage and the sea, to watch the people gathering carragheen moss, a trade which is much followed in this district during the spring tides of summer. I lay down on the edge of the cliff, where the heathery hill comes to an end and the steep rocks begin. About a mile to the west there was a long headland, 'Feakle Callaigh' ('The Witch's Tooth'), covered with mists, that blew over me from time to time with a swish of rain, followed by sunshine again. The mountains on the other side of the bay were covered, so I could see nothing but the strip of brilliant sea below me, thronged with girls and men up to their waists in the water, with a hamper in one hand and a stick in the other, gathering the moss, and talking and laughing loudly as they worked. The long frill of dark golden rocks covered with seaweed, with the asses and children slipping about on it, and the bars of silvery light breaking through on the further inlets of the bay, had the singularly brilliant liveliness one meets everywhere in Kerry.

When the tide began to come in I went down one of the passes to the sea, and met many

parties of girls and old men and women coming
up with what they had gathered, most of them
still wearing the clothes that had been in the sea,
and were heavy and black with salt water. A
little further on I met Danny-boy and we sat
down to talk.

'Do you see that sandy head?' he said, pointing out to the east, 'that is called the Stooks of
the Dead Women; for one time a boat came
ashore there with twelve dead women on board
her, big ladies with green dresses and gold rings,
and fine jewelries, and a dead harper or fiddler
along with them. Then there are graves again in
the little hollow by the cnuceen, and what we
call them is the Graves of the Sailors; for some
sailors, Greeks or great strangers, were washed in
there a hundred years ago, and it is there that
they were buried.'

Then we began talking of the carragheen he
had gathered and the spring-tides that would
come again during the summer. I took out my
diary to tell him the times of the moon, but he
would hardly listen to me. When I stopped he
gave his ass a cut with his stick, 'Go on, now,' he
said; 'I wouldn't believe those almanacks at all;
they do not tell the truth about the moon.'

The greatest event in West Kerry is the horse-fair, known as Puck Fair, which is held in August. If one asks anyone, many miles east or west of Killorglin, when he reaped his oats or sold his pigs or heifers, he will tell you it was four or five weeks, or whatever it may be, before or after Puck. On the main roads, for many days past, I have been falling in with tramps and trick characters of all kinds, sometimes single and sometimes in parties of four or five, and as I am on the roads a great deal I have often met the same persons several days in succession — one day perhaps at Ballinskelligs, the next day at Feakle Callaigh, and the third in the outskirts of Killorglin.

Yesterday cavalcades of every sort were passing from the west with droves of horses, mares, jennets, foals and asses, with their owners going after them in flat or railed carts, or riding on ponies.

The men of this house — they are going to buy a horse — went to the fair last night, and I followed at an early hour in the morning. As I came near Killorglin the road was much blocked by the latest sellers pushing eagerly forward, and early purchasers who were anxiously leading off their young horses before the roads became

dangerous from the crush of drunken drivers and
riders.

Just outside the town, near the first public-
house, blind beggars were kneeling on the pathway, praying with almost Oriental volubility for
the souls of anyone who would throw them a
coin.

'May the Holy Immaculate Mother of Jesus
Christ,' said one of them, 'intercede for you in
the hour of need. Relieve a poor blind creature,
and may Jesus Christ relieve yourselves in the
hour of death. May He have mercy, I'm saying,
on your brothers and fathers and sisters for
evermore.'

Further on stalls were set out with cheap
cakes and refreshments, and one could see that
many houses had been arranged to supply the
crowds who had come in. Then I came to the
principal road that goes round the fair-green,
where there was a great concourse of horses,
trotting and walking and galloping; most of
them were of the cheaper class of animal, and
were selling, apparently to the people's satisfaction, at prices that reminded one of the time
when fresh meat was sold for three pence a
pound. At the further end of the green there
were one or two rough shooting galleries, and a

number of women — not very rigid, one could
see — selling, or appearing to sell, all kinds of
trifles: a set that come in, I am told, from towns
not far away. At the end of the green I turned
past the chapel, where a little crowd had just
carried in a man who had been killed or badly
wounded by a fall from a horse, and went down
to the bridge of the river, and then back again
into the main slope of the town. Here there were
a number of people who had come in for amusement only, and were walking up and down,
looking at each other — a crowd is as exciting as
champagne to these lonely people, who live in
long glens among the mountains — and meeting
with cousins and friends. Then, in the three-
cornered space in the middle of the town, I
came on Puck himself, a magnificent he-goat
(Irish puc), raised on a platform twenty feet
high, and held by a chain from each horn, with
his face down the road. He is kept in this
position, with a few cabbages to feed on, for
three days, so that he may preside over the pig-
fair and the horse-fair and the day of winding up.

At the foot of this platform, where the crowd
was thickest, a young ballad-singer was howling-
ing a ballad in honour of Puck, making one
think of the early Greek festivals, since the time

of which, it is possible, the goat has been exalted yearly in Killorglin.

The song was printed in on a green slip by itself. It ran:—

A NEW SONG ON THE GREAT PUCK FAIR
By JOHN PURCELL

All young lovers that are fond of sporting, pay
    attention for a while,
I will sing you the praises of Puck Fair, and I'm
    sure it will make you smile;
Where the lads and lassies coming gaily to
    Killorglin can be seen,
To view the Puck upon the stage, as our hero
    dressed in green.

Chorus
    And hurra for the gallant Puck so gay,
    For he is a splendid one:
    Wind and rain don't touch his tail,
    For his hair is thirty inches long.

Now it is on the square he's erected with all
    colours grand and gay;
There's not a fair throughout Ireland, but Puck
    Fair it takes the sway,
Where you see the gamblers in rotation, trick-o'-
    the-loop and other games,

The ballad-singers and the wheel of fortune and
   the shooting-gallery for to take aim.

Chorus

Where is the tyrant dare oppose it?
Our old customs we will hold up still,
And I think we will have another —
That is, Home Rule and Purchase Bill.

Now, all young men that are not married, next
   Shrove can take a wife,
For before next Puck Fair we will have Home
   Rule, and then you will be settled down in life.
Now the same advice I give young girls for to
   get married and have pluck.
Let the landlords see that you defy them when
   coming to Fair of Puck.

Cead Mile Failte to the Fair of Puck.

When one makes the obvious elisions, the
lines are not so irregular as they look, and are
always sung to a measure; yet the whole, in spite
of the assonance, rhymes, and the 'colours grand
and gay' seems pitifully remote from any good
spirit of ballad-making.

Across the square, a man and a woman, who
had a baby tied on her back, were singing another
ballad on the Russian and Japanese War, in the

curious method of antiphony that is still sometimes heard in the back streets of Dublin. These
are some of the verses:—

Man

Now provisions are rising, 'tis sad for to state,
The flour, tea and sugar, tobacco and meat;
But, God help us! poor Irish, how must we stand
    the test

Ambo

If they only now stop the trade of commerce.

Woman

Now the Russians are powerful on sea and on
    land;
But the Japs they are active, they will them
    command,
Before this war is finished I have one word to
    say,

Ambo

There will be more shot and drowned than in
    the Crimea.

Man

Now the Japs are victorious up to this time,
And thousands of Russians I hear they are dying.
        Etc., etc.

And so it went on with the same alternation
of the voices through seven or eight verses; and

it was curious to feel how much was gained by
this simple variation of the voices.

When I passed back to the fair-green, I met
the men I am staying with, and went off with
them under an archway, and into a back yard to
look at a little two-year-old filly that they had
bought and left for the moment in a loose box
with three or four young horses. She was prettily
and daintily shaped, but looked too light, I
thought, for the work she will be expected to
do. As we came out again into the road, an old
man was singing an out-spoken ballad on women
in the middle of the usual crowd. Just as we
passed it came to a scandalous conclusion; and
the women scattered in every direction, shrieking with laughter and holding shawls over their
mouths.

At the corner we turned into a public-house,
where there were men we knew, who had done
their business also; and we went into the little
alcove to sit down quietly for a moment. 'What
will you take, sir;' said the man I lodge with, 'a
glass of wine?'

I took beer and the others took porter; but
we were only served after some little time, as the
house was thronged with people.

The men were too much taken up with their

bargains and losses to talk much of other matters; and before long we came out again, and the son of the house started homewards, leading the new filly by a little halter of rope.

Not long afterwards I started also. Outside Killorglin rain was coming up over the hills of Glen Car, so that there was a strained hush in the air, and a rich, aromatic smell coming from the bog myrtle, or boggy shrub, that grows thickly in this place. The strings of horses and jennets scattered over the road did not keep away a strange feeling of loneliness that seems to hang over this brown plain of bog that stretches from Carrantuohill to Cuchulain's House.

Before I reached the cottage dense torrents of rain were closing down through the glens, and driving in white sheets between the little hills that are on each side of the way.

One morning in autumn I started in a local train for the first stage of my journey to Dublin, seeing the last of Macgillicuddy's Reeks, that were touched with snow in places, Dingle Bay and the islands beyond it. At a little station where I changed trains, I got into a carriage where there was a woman with her daughter, a girl of about twenty, who seemed uneasy and

distressed. Soon afterwards, when a collector
was looking at our tickets, I called out that mine
was for Dublin, and as soon as he got out the
woman came over to me.

'Are you going to Dublin?' she said.

I told her I was.

'Well,' she went on, 'here is my daughter
going there too; and maybe you'd look after her,
for I'm getting down at the next station. She is
going up to a hospital for some little complaint
in her ear, and she has never travelled before, so
that she's lonesome in her mind.'

I told her I would do what I could, and at
the next station I was left alone with my charge,
and one other passenger, a returned American
girl, who was on her way to Mallow, to get the
train for Queenstown. When her mother was
lost sight of the young girl broke out into tears,
and the returned American and myself had
trouble to quiet her.

'Look at me,' said the American. 'I'm going
off for ten years to America, all by myself, and
I don't care a rap.'

When the girl got quiet again, the returned
American talked to me about scenery and
politics and the arts — she had been seen off by
her sisters in bare feet, with shawls over their

heads — and the life of women in America.

At several stations girls and boys thronged in to get places for Queenstown, leaving parties of old men and women wailing with anguish on the platform. At one place an old woman was seized with such a passion of regret, when she saw her daughters moving away from her for ever, that she made a wild rush after the train; and when I looked out for a moment I could see her writhing and struggling on the platform, with her hair over her face, and two men holding her by the arms.

Two young men had got into our compartment for a few stations only, and they looked on with the greatest satisfaction.

'Ah,' said one of them, 'we do have great sport every Friday and Saturday, seeing the old women howling in the stations.'

When we reached Dublin I left my charge for a moment to see after my baggage, and when I came back I found her sitting on a luggage barrow, with her package in her hand, crying with despair because several cabmen had refused to let her into their cabs, on the pretext that they dreaded infection.

I could see they were looking out for some rich tourist with his trunks, as a more lucrative fare; so I sent for the head-porter, who had charge of the platform. When the porter arrived we chose a cab, and I saw my charge driven off to her hospital, sitting on the front seat, with her handkerchief to her eyes.

For the last few days — I am staying in the Kerry cottage I have spoken of already — the people have been talking of horse-races that were to be held on the sand, not far off, and this morning I set out to see them with the man and woman of the house and two of their neighbours. Our way led through a steep boreen for a quarter of a mile to the edge of the sea, and then along a pathway between the cliffs and a straight grassy hill. When we had gone some distance the old man pointed out a slope in front of us, where, he said, Diarmuid had done his tricks of rolling the barrel and jumping over his spear, and had killed many of his enemies. He told me the whole story, slightly familiarised in detail, but not very different from the version everyone knows. A little further on he pointed across the sea to our left — just beyond the strand where the races were to be run — to a neck of sand where, he said, Oisin was called away to the Tir-na-nOg.

'The Tir-na-nOg itself,' he said, 'is below that
sea, and a while since there were two men out in
a boat in the night-time, and they got stuck outside some way or another. They went to sleep
then, and when one of them wakened up he
looked down into the sea, and he saw the Tir-
na-nOg and people walking about, and side-cars
driving in the squares.'

Then he began telling me stories of mermaids
— a common subject in this neighbourhood.

'There was one time a man beyond of the
name of Shee,' he said, 'and his master seen a
mermaid on the sand beyond combing her hair,
and he told Shee to get her. "I will," said Shee,
"if you'll give me the best horse you have in
your stable." "I'll do that," said the master.
Then Shee got the horse, and when he saw the
mermaid on the sand combing her hair, with her
covering laid away from ner, he galloped up,
when she wasn't looking, and he picked up the
covering and away he went with it. Then the
waves rose up behind him and he galloped his
best, and just as he was coming out at the top
of the tide the ninth wave cut off his horse
behind his back, and left himself and the half
of his horse and the covering on the dry land.
Then the mermaid came in after her covering,

and the master got married to her, and she lived
with him a long time, and had children — three
or four of them. Well, in the wind-up, the master
built a fine new house, and when he was moving
into it, and clearing the things out, he brought
down an old hamper out of the loft and put it in
the yard. The woman was going about, and she
looked into the hamper, and she saw her covering hidden away in the bottom of it. She took it
out then and put it upon her and went back into
the sea, and her children used to be on the shore
crying after her. I'm told from that day there
isn't one of the Shees can go out in a boat on
that bay and not be drowned.'

We were now near the sandhills, where a
crowd was beginning to come together, and
booths were being put up for the sale of apples
and porter and cakes. A train had come in a
little before at a station a mile or so away, and a
number of the usual trick-characters, with their
stock-in-trade, were hurrying down to the sea.
The roulette man passed us first, unfolding his
table and calling out at the top of his voice:

Come play me a game of timmun and tup,
The more you puts down the more you takes
up.

'Take notice, gentlemen, I come here to spend

a fortune, not to make one. Is there any sports-
man in a hat or a cap, or a wig or a waistcoat,
will play a go with me now? Take notice, gentlemen, the luck is on the green.'

The races had to be run between two tides
while the sand was dry, so there was not much
time to be lost, and before we reached the
strand the horses had been brought together,
ridden by young men in many variations of
jockey dress. For the first race there was one
genuine race-horse, very old and bony, and two
or three young horses belonging to farmers in
the neighbourhood. The start was made from
the middle of the crowd at the near end of the
strand, and the course led out along the edge of
the sea to a post some distance away, back again
to the starting-point, round a post, and out and
back once more.

When the word was given the horses set off in
a wild helter-skelter along the edge of the sea,
with crowds cheering them on from the sandhills.
As they got small in the distance it was not easy
to see which horse was leading, but after a sort
of check, as they turned the post, they began
nearing again a few yards from the waves, with
the old race-horse, heavily pressed, a good length
ahead. The stewards made a sort of effort to

clear the post that was to be circled, but without much success, as the people were wild with excitement. A moment later the old race-horse galloped into the crowd, twisted too suddenly, something cracked and jolted, and it limped out on three legs, gasping with pain. The next horse could not be stopped, and galloped out at the wrong end of the crowd for some little way before it could be brought back, so the last horses set off in front for the final lap.

The lame race-horse was now mobbed by on-lookers and advisers, talking incoherently.

'Was it the fault of the jock?' said one man.

'It was not,' said another, 'for Michael (the owner) didn't strike him, and if it had been his fault, wouldn't he have broken his bones?'

'He was striving to spare a young girl had run out in his way,' said another. 'It was for that he twisted him.'

'Little slut!' said a woman; 'what did she want beyond on the sand?'

Many remedies were suggested that did not sound reassuring, and in the end the horse was led off in a hopeless condition. A little later the race ended with an easy win for the wildest of the young horses. Afterwards I wandered up among the people, and looked at the sports. At one place a man, with his face heavily blackened, except one cheek and eye — an extraordinary effect — was standing shots of a wooden ball behind a board with a large hole in the middle, at three shots a penny. When I came past half an hour afterwards he had been hit in the mouth — by a girl some one told me — but seemed as cheerful as ever.

On the road, some little distance away, a party of girls and young men were dancing polkas to the music of a melodeon, in a cloud of dust. When I had looked on for a little while I met some girls I knew, and asked them how they were getting on.

'We're not getting on at all,' said one of them, 'for we've been at the races for two hours, and we've found no beaux to go along with us.'

When the horses had all run, a jennet race was held, and greatly delighted the people, as the jennets — there were a number of them — got scared by the cheering and ran wild in every direction. In the end it was not easy to say which was the winner, and a dispute began which nearly ended in blows. It was decided at last to run the race over again the following Sunday after Mass, so everyone was satisfied.

The day was magnificently bright, and the ten

miles of Dingle Bay were wonderfully brilliant behind the masses of people, and the canvas booths, and the scores of upturned shafts. Towards evening I got tired taking or refusing the porter my friends pressed on me continually, so I wandered off from the racecourse along the path where Diarmuid had tricked the Fenians.

Later in the evening news had been coming in of the doings in the sandhills, after the porter had begun to take effect and the darkness had come on.

'There was great sport after you left,' a man said to me in the cottage this evening. 'They were all beating and cutting each other on the shore of the sea. Four men fought together in one place till the tide came up on them, and was like to drown them; but the priest waded out up to his middle and drove them asunder. Another man was left for dead on the road outside the lodges, and some gentleman found him and had him carried into his house, and got the doctor to put plasters on his head. Then there was a red-headed fellow had his finger bitten through, and the postman was destroyed for ever.'

'He should be,' said the man of the house, 'for Michael Patch broke the seat of his car into three halves on his head.'

'It was this was the cause of it all,' said Danny-
boy: 'they brought in porter east and west from
the two towns you know of, and the two porters
didn't agree together, and it's for that the people
went raging at the fall of night.'

I have been out to Bolus Head, one of the
finest places I have met with. A little beyond
Ballinskelligs the road turns up the side of a
steep mountainy hill where one sees a brilliant
stretch of sea, with many rocks and islands —
Deenish, Scariff, the Hog's Head, and Dursey far
away. As I was sitting on the edge of the road an
old man came along and we began to talk. He
had little English, but when I tried him in Irish
we got on well, though he did not follow any
Connaught forms I let slip by accident. We went
on together, after a while, to an extraordinary
straggling village along the edge of the hill. At
one of the cottages he stopped and asked me to
come in and take a drink and rest myself. I did
not like to refuse him, we had got so friendly, so
I followed him in, and sat down on a stool while
his wife — a much younger woman — went into
the bedroom and brought me a large mug of
milk. As I was drinking it and talking to the

couple, a sack that was beside the fire began to move slowly, and the head of a yellow, feverish-looking child came out from beneath it, and began looking at me with a heavy stare. I asked the woman what ailed it, and she told me it had sickened a night or two before with headache and pains all through it; but she had not had the doctor, and did not know what was the matter. I finished the milk without much enjoyment, and went on my way up Bolus Head and then back to this cottage, wondering all the time if I had the germs of typhus in my blood.

Last night, when I got back to the cottage, I found that another 'travelling man' had arrived to stay for a day or two; but he was hard of hearing and a little simple in his head, so that we had not much talk. I went to bed soon after dark and slept till about two o'clock in the morning, when I was awakened by fearful screams in the kitchen. For a moment I did not know where I was; then I remembered the old man, and I jumped up and went to the door of my room. As I opened it I heard the door of the family room across the kitchen opening also, and the frightened whispers of the people. In a moment we could hear the old man, who was sleeping on the settle, pulling himself out of a nightmare, so we went back to our beds.

In the morning the woman told me his story:

'He was living above on a little hillside,' she said, 'in a bit of a cabin, with his sister along with him. Then, after a while, she got ailing in her heart, and he got a bottle for her from the doctor, and he'd rise up every morning before the dawn to give her a sup of it. She got better then, till one night he got up and measured out the spoonful, or whatever it was, and went to give it to her, and he found her stretched out dead before him. Since that night he wakes up one time and another, and begins crying out for Maurya — that was his sister — and he half in his dreams. It was that you heard in the night, and indeed it would frighten any person to hear him screaming as if he was getting his death.'

When the little man came back after a while, they began asking him questions till he told his whole story, weeping pitiably. Then they got him to tell me about the other great event of his life also, in the rather childish Gaelic he uses.

He had once a little cur-dog, he said, and he knew nothing of the dog licence; then one day the peelers — the boys with the little caps — asked him into the barracks for a cup of tea. He went in cheerfully, and then they put him and his little dog into the lock-up till someone paid a shilling for him and got him out.

He has a stick he is proud of, bound with pieces of leather every few inches — like one I have seen with a beggar in Belmullet. Since the first night he has not had nightmare again, and he lies most of the evening sleeping on the settle, and in the morning he goes round among the houses, getting his share of meal and potatoes.

I do not think a beggar is ever refused in Kerry. Sometimes, while we are talking or doing something in the kitchen, a man walks in without saying anything and stands just inside the door, with his bag on the floor beside him. In five or ten minutes, when the woman of the house has finished what she is doing, she goes up to him and asks: 'Is it meal or flour?' 'Flour,' says the man. She goes into the inner room, opens her sack, and comes back with two handfuls. He opens his bag and takes out a bundle carefully tied up in a cloth or handkerchief; he opens this again, and usually there is another cloth inside, into which the woman puts her flour. Then the cloths are carefully knotted together by the corners, put back in the bag, and the man mutters a 'God bless you,' and goes on his way.

The meal, flour and potatoes that are thus
gathered up are always sold by the beggar, and
the money is spent on porter or second-hand
clothes, or very occasionally on food when he is
in a neighbourhood that is not hospitable. The
buyers are usually found among the coast-
guards' wives, or in the little public-houses on
the roadside.

'Some of these men,' said the woman of the
house, when I asked her about them, 'will take
their flour nicely and tastily and cleanly, and
others will throw it in anyway, and you'd be
sorry to eat it afterwards.'

The talk of these people is almost bewildering.
I have come to this cottage again and again, and
I often think I have heard all they have to say,
and then someone makes a remark that leads to
a whole new bundle of folk-tales, or stories of
wonderful events that have happened in the
barony in the last hundred years. Tonight the
people were unusually silent, although several
neighbours had come in, and to make conver-
sation I said something about the bull-fights in
Spain that I had been reading of in the news-
papers. Immediately they started off with stories
of wicked or powerful bulls, and then they
branched off to clever dogs and all the things

they have done in West Kerry, and then to mad
dogs and mad cattle and pigs — one incident
after another, but always detailed and picturesque and interesting.

I have come back to the north of Dingle,
leaving Tralee late in the afternoon. At the
station there was a more than usually great
crowd, as there had been a fair in the town and
many people had come in to make their Saturday purchases. A number of messenger boys
with parcels from the shops in the town were
shouting for the owners, using many familiar
names, Justin MacCarthy, Hannah Lynch and
the like. I managed to get a seat on a sack of
flour beside the owner, who had other packages
scattered under our feet. When the train had
started and the women and girls — the carriage
was filled with them — had settled down into
their places, I could see I caused great curiosity,
as it was too late in the year for even an odd
tourist, and on this line everyone is known by
sight.

Before long I got into talk with the old man
next me, and as soon as I did so the women and
girls stopped their talk and leaned out to hear
what we were saying.

He asked first if I belonged to Dingle, and I told him I did not.

'Well,' he said, 'you speak like a Kerry man, and you're dressed like a Kerry man, so you belong to Kerry surely.'

I told him I was born and bred in Dublin, and that I had travelled in many places in Ireland and beyond it.

'That's easy said,' he answered, 'but I'd take an oath you were never beyond Kerry to this day.'

Then he asked sharply:— 'What do you do?'

I answered something about my wanderings in Europe, and suddenly he sat up, as if a new thought had come to him.

'Maybe you're a wealthy man?' he said.

I smiled complacently.

'And about thirty-five?'

I nodded.

'And not married?'

'No.'

'Well, then,' he said, 'you're a damn lucky fellow to be travelling the world with no one to impede you.'

Then he went on to discuss the expenses of travelling.

'You'll likely be paying twenty pounds for this trip,' he said, 'with getting your lodging and buying your tickets, till you're back in the city of Dublin?'

I told him my expenses were not so heavy.

'Maybe you don't drink so,' said his wife, who was near us, 'and that way your living wouldn't be so costly at all.'

An interruption was made by a stop at a small station and the entrance of a ragged ballad-singer, who sang a long ballad about the sorrows of mothers who see all their children going away from them to America.

Further on, when the carriage was much emptier, a middle-aged man got in, and we began discussing the fishing season, Aran fishing, hookers, nobbies and mackerel. I could see, while we were talking, that he, in his turn, was examining me with curiosity. At last he seemed satisfied.

'Begob,' he said, 'I see what you are; you're a fish-dealer.'

It turned out that he was the skipper of a trawler, and we had a long talk, the two of us and a local man who was going to Dingle also.

'There was one time a Frenchman below,' said the skipper, 'who got married here and settled down and worked with the rest of us. One day we were outside in the trawler, and there was a French boat anchored a bit of a way off. "Come on," says Charley — that was his name — "and see can we get some brandy from that boat beyond." "How would we get brandy," says I, "when we've no fish, or meat, or cabbages or a thing at all to offer them?" He went down below then to see what he could get. At that time there were four men only working the trawler, and in the heavy season there were eight. Well, up he comes again and eight plates under his arm. "There are eight plates," says he, "and four will do us; so we'll take out the other four and make a swap with them for brandy." With that he set the eight plates on the deck and began walking up and down and looking on them.

' "The devil mend you," says I. "Will you take them up and come on, if you're coming?"

' "I will," says he, "surely. I'm choicing out the ones that have pictures on them, for it's that kind they do set store on." '

Afterwards we began talking of boats that had been upset during the winter, and lives that had been lost in the neighbourhood.

'A while since,' said the local man, 'there were three men out in a canoe, and the sea rose on them. They tried to come in under the cliff, but they couldn't come to land with the greatness of

the waves that were breaking. There were two
young men in the canoe, and another man was
sixty, or near it. When the young men saw they
couldn't bring in the canoe, they said they'd
make a jump for the rocks and let her go without them, if she must go. Then they pulled in on
the next wave, and when they were close in the
two young men jumped on to a rock, but the
old man was too stiff, and he was washed back
again in the canoe. It came on dark after that,
and all thought he was drowned, and they held
his wake in Dunquin. At that time there used to
be a steamer going in and out trading in Valentia
and Dingle and Cahirciveen, and when she came
into Dingle, two or three days after, there was
my man on board her, as hearty as a salmon.
When he was washed back he got one of the oars,
and kept her head to the wind; then the tide
took him one bit and the wind took him another,
and he wrought and he wrought till he was safe
beyond in Valentia. Wasn't that a great wonder?'
Then as he was ending his story we ran down
into Dingle.

Often, when one comes back to a place that
one's memory and imagination have been busy
with, there is a feeling of smallness and dis-

appointment, and it is a day or two before one can renew all one's enjoyment. This morning, however, when I went up the gap between Croagh Martin and then back to Slea Head, and saw Innishtooskert and Inishvickillaun and the Great Blasket Island itself, they seemed ten times more grey and wild and magnificent than anything I had kept in my memory. The cold sea and surf, and the feeling of winter in the clouds, and the blackness of the rocks, and the red fern everywhere, were a continual surprise and excitement.

Here and there on my way I met old men with tail-coats of frieze, that are becoming so uncommon. When I spoke to them in English they shook their heads and muttered something I could not hear; but when I tried Irish they made me long speeches about the weather and the clearness of the day.

In the evening, as I was coming home, I got a glimpse that seemed to have the whole character of Corkaguiney — a little line of low cottages with yellow roofs, and an elder tree without leaves beside them, standing out against a high mountain that seemed far away, yet was near enough to be dense and rich and wonderful in its colour.

Then I wandered round the wonderful forts of Fahan. The blueness of the sea and the hills from Carrantuohill to the Skelligs, the singular loneliness of the hillside I was on, with a few choughs and gulls in sight only, had a splendour that was almost a grief in the mind.

I turned into a little public-house this evening, where Maurice — the fisherman I have spoken of before — and some of his friends often sit when it is too wild for fishing. While we were talking a man came in, and joined rather busily in what was being said, though I could see he was not belonging to the place. He moved his position several times till he was quite close to me, then he whispered: 'Will you stand me a medium, mister? I'm hard set for money this while past.' When he had got his medium he began to give me his history. He was a journeyman tailor who had been a year or more in the place, and was beginning to pick up a little Irish to get along with. When he had gone we had a long talk about the making of canoes and the difference between those used in Connaught and Munster.

'They have been in this country,' said Maurice, 'for twenty or twenty-five years only, and before that we had boats; a canoe will cost

twelve pounds, or maybe thirteen pounds, and
there is one old man beyond who charges fifteen
pounds. If it is well done a canoe will stand for
eight years, and you can get a new skin on it
when the first one is gone.'

I told him I thought canoes had been in
Connemara since the beginning of the world.

'That may well be,' he went on, 'for there was
a certain man going out as a pilot, up and down
into Clare, and it was he made them first in this
place. It is a trade few can learn, for it is all done
within the head; you will have to sit down and
think it out, and then make up when it is all
ready in your mind.'

I described the fixed thole-pins that are used
in Connaught — here they use two freely moving
thole-pins, with the oar loose between them, and
they jeered at the simplicity of the Connaught
system. Then we got on the relative value of
canoes and boats.

'They are not better than boats,' said Maurice,
'but they are more useful. Before you get a
heavy boat swimming you will be wet up to
your waist, and then you will be sitting the
whole night like that; but a canoe will swim in
a handful of water, so that you can get in dry
and be dry and warm the whole night. Then

there will be seven men in a big boat and seven shares of the fish; but in a canoe there will be three men only and three shares of the fish, though the nets are the same in the two.'

After a while a man sang a song, and then we began talking of tunes and playing the fiddle, and I told them how hard it was to get any sound out of one in a cottage with a floor of earth and a thatched roof over you.

'I can believe that,' said one of the men. 'There was a man a while since went into Tralee to buy a fiddle; and when he went into the shop an old fiddler followed him into it, thinking maybe he'd get the price of a pint. Well, the man was within choicing the fiddles, maybe forty of them, and the old fiddler whispered to him to take them out into the air, "for there's many a fiddle would sound well in here wouldn't be worth a curse outside," says he; so he was bringing them out and bringing them out till he found a good one among them.'

This evening, after a day of teeming rain, it cleared for an hour, and I went out while the sun was setting to a little cove where a high sea was running. As I was coming back the darkness began to close in except in the west, where there

was a red light under the clouds. Against this
light I could see patches of open wall and little
fields of stooks, and a bit of laneway with an old
man driving white cows before him. These
seemed transfigured beyond any description.

Then I passed two men riding bare-backed
towards the west, who spoke to me in Irish, and
a little further on I came to the only village on
my way. The ground rose towards it, and as I
came near there was a grey bar of smoke from
every cottage going up to the low clouds over-
head, and standing out strangely against the
blackness of the mountain behind the village.

Beyond the patch of wet cottages I had
another stretch of lonely roadway, and a heron
kept flapping in front of me, rising and lighting
again with many lonely cries that made me glad
to reach the little public-house near Smerwick.

MORE MERCIER BESTSELLERS

IN CONNEMARA
John M. Synge

Our breathless interest is sustained throughout this fascinating book as J.M. Synge shows us that 'one has to go a little way only to reach places and people that are typical of Connemara'. He paints a very moving picture of the reality of rural life in the west of Ireland. He admires the the simplicity of the peoples' character, their skill in many varied crafts and their readiness to face risks and danger without any show of bravado. We hear the call of the wild and our professors are the fishermen, mountainy men and the people of the bogs. Synge's sympathy and delight with whatever was traditional enriches every page of this book. As we visit Spiddal, Carraroe, Ballina, Belmullet and the inner lands of Mayo we frequently hear beautiful and striking phrases as we meet the fiery and magnificent peasants in their cottages.

It is a little star-dust caught, a segment of the rainbow which I have clutched.

THE WIND THAT ROUND THE FASTNET SWEEPS
John M. Feehan

There are moments in the life of every human being when he becomes haunted with the longing to leave behind the turmoil and tension of daily living, to get away from it all and to escape to a clime where true peace can be found. There are many practical reasons why most of us cannot do this so the next best thing is to read the story of one who tried.

John M. Feehan sailed, all by himself, in a small boat around the coast of West Cork in a search for this Land of the Heart's Desire, this Isle of the Blest.

The result is a book which is not only a penetrating spiritual odyssey, but also a magnificent account of the wild rugged coastline, the peaceful harbours, and the strange unique characters he met in this unspoiled corner of Ireland. He writes with great charm, skill, sympathy and a mischievous roguish humour often at his own expense. His sharp eye misses nothing. He sees the mystery, the beauty and the sense of wonder in ordinary things, and brings each situation to life so that the reader feels almost physically present during every moment of the cruise. *'...brilliant... the Irish Story of San Michele.'* — *John.B. Keane.*

THE MAGIC OF THE KERRY COAST
J.M. Feehan

This is a sequel to the best selling *The Wind That Round the Fastnet Sweeps*. In it John M. Feehan continues his odyssey from Crookhaven

up the coast of Kerry to the Skellig Rocks and the Blasket Islands. It follows the same pattern — a little sailing, a little thinking, a little laughing, a little drinking and once again we meet a marvellous collection of those strange and unusual characters who always seem to run across the author's path and which he describes with such understanding and humanity.
(June 1979).

RAMBLES IN THE WEST OF IRELAND
William Bulfin
William Bulfin takes us on a fascinating journey through the west of Ireland and we see haymaking, turf-cutting and enjoy a chat with the old people and listen to their stories. The reader will feel the pleasure of standing beside the graves of heroes and the ground made sacred by their heroism and will delight in visiting the banks of the Shannon. While reading this fascinating book it will be hard to remain in the present time as our thoughts will be far away while travelling the winding roads.

LETTERS FROM THE GREAT BLASKET
Eibhlis Ni Shulleabhain
A fascinating story of a strange and different way of life emerges in these letters which deal with the Great Blasket Island, its people and its

ways. They also include what must be an almost unique specimen of 'The Islandman's' writing in English.

THE MAN FROM CAPE CLEAR
Conchur O Siochain
Translated by Riobard P. Breatnach

Conchur O Siochain lived all his days on Cape Clear, the southern outpost of an old and deep-rooted civilisation. He lived as a farmer and as a fisherman and his story portrays the life of the island (Fastnet Rock's nearest neighbour). He was a gifted man in many ways and developed skills as a storyteller, a folklorist and a craftsman. The book is a collection of memories and musings, topography and tales, descriptions of old ways and crafts, and contains a fund of seafaring yarns and lore.

The Man from Cape Clear has been acclaimed as a greater book than *The Islandman*.

SUPERSTITIONS OF THE IRISH COUNTRY PEOPLE
Padraic O'Farrell

A Collection of Ireland's best known superstitions: Do you know why it is considered unlucky to meet a barefooted man, to start out on a journey on the tenth of November, to get married on a Saturday?

Irish country people believe that angels are always present among them and that all good things — crops, rain and so forth come from them. Bad spirits bring sickness to humans and animals and pestilence to crops. They do not speak of fairies on Wednesdays or Fridays for on those days they could be present while still being invisible.

THE YEAR IN IRELAND—
Irish Calendar Custom
Kevin Danaher

This beautiful book describes how the round of the year, with its cycle of festivals and seasonal work was observed in the Ireland of yesterday.

History of the Name Murphy
J.D. Williams

History of the Name O'Sullivan
J.D. Williams

History of the Name O'Neill
J.D. Williams

History of the Name MacCarthy
J.D. Williams

History of the Name O'Brien
J.D. Williams

History of the Name O'Kelly
J.D. Williams

Here for the first time is a popular series of books on Irish surnames written for the Irish and those of Irish extraction who want to know more about their heritage. Each book is divided into two sections, the first a detailed study of the history of Irish surnames and the second the history of the particular surname, and they look at some of the famous people throughout the world who hold the surname.

MALACHI HORAN REMEMBERS
Dr. G. Little

Malachi Horan Remembers is real and stirring history caught from living lips, just in time to save a hundred quaint, beautiful, precious things from oblivion. The book is a revelation. It describes authentically a purely Irish, robust, picturesque life, like that of unspoilt Donegal, Connacht or Kerry — thriving in the life-time and of the teller, on the hills that can be seen from Dublin's streets. Hedge schools, wooden ploughs drawn by bullock teams, fairy lore, quaint folktales, unique relics of Leinster Irish, road tolls — all are described by one who knew them. County Dublin, we see here, is truly an Irish-Ireland, too.

'This is a darling book. The general reader will devour it for sheer delight. The folklorist already has pronounced it a treasure.'

IN IRELAND LONG AGO
Kevin Danaher

Kevin Danaher describes life in Ireland before the 'brave new world' crept into the quiet countryside. Or perhaps 'describe' is not the right word. He rather invites the reader to call on the elderly people at their homes, to listen to their tales and gossip and taste their food and drink; to step outside and marvel at their pots and pans, ploughs and flails; to meet a water diviner; to join a faction fight; hurry to a wedding and bow down in remembrance of the dead.

IRISH FAIRY TALES
Edmund Leamy

In writing these spell-binding tales Edmund Leamy turned to our Gaelic past to give to the Irish people something that would implant in them a love for the beauty and dignity of their country's traditions.

IRISH GHOST STORIES
Patrick F. Byrne

There is a strong and ancient tradition of ghosts in Ireland. While many of the tales are obvious figments of imagination, there are certain stories which cannot be explained away.

The author has probed deeply into many of these spooky goings-on in all parts of the country, and relates his findings here.

Perhaps the most horrifying stories refer to the 'Hungry Grass', a product of the unspeakable horror left in people's minds by the Famine. It grows where a victim of the Famine perished; and to cross it at night is to be seized with a hunger which causes death if not immediately satisfied.

THE SECOND BOOK OF IRISH GHOST STORIES
Patrick Byrne

As the author says in his introduction there seems to be an unending stream of tales of the supernatural in this country, and here are more uncanny tales.

IRISH GHOST STORIES OF LE FANU
Patrick Byrne

Urbane, witty and absolutely terrifying, these ghost stories are as much a pleasure to read today as they have been to his readers for more than a century since their original publication. The stories in this book, long out of print, are set in and around a bygone Dublin which Le Fanu so vividly evokes.

THE BOOK OF IRISH CURSES
Patrick C. Power

The Book of Irish Curses is an extremely interesting, well written, fascinating and entertaining book. It is a remarkable blend of history, folklore and anecdote. The author deals at length with the types of Irish curses, their age and styles, their rituals, and concludes with a do-it-yourself cursing kit.

THE FARM BY LOUGH GUR
Mary Carbery

This is the true story of a family who lived on a farm by Lough Gur, the Enchanted Lake, in Co. Limerick. The story is also a picture of manners and customs in a place so remote that religion had still to reckon with pagan survivals, where a fairy-doctor cured the landlord's bewitched cows, and a banshee comforted the dying with the music of harps and flutes.

THE FIRST BOOK OF IRISH MYTHS AND LEGENDS
Eoin Neeson

Eoin Neeson delves deep into the past and comes up with plenty of intrigue, romance and excitement in these stories about our ancestors.

THE SECOND BOOK OF IRISH MYTHS AND LEGENDS
Eoin Neeson

Again more fascinating legends from Eoin Neeson. Included are: 'The Children of Lir', the classic tale of 'Diarmuid and Grainne' and an unusual tale about 'Cuchulainn'.